THE DEBATE OVER SENIORITY AND AFFIRMATIVE ACTION

By Linda Jenness

The rise of the civil rights and women's liberation movements in the 1960s spurred many battles against discrimination in hiring and promotions. Women and Blacks and other oppressed nationalities scored some victories in breaking into higher-paying positions long denied them because of racist and sexist practices.

Much of the hiring and job upgrading for women and minorities was the result of affirmative-action plans, often won through lawsuits. In essence these plans amounted to preferential hiring, or quotas, to begin to correct the gross inequities faced by women and Blacks in the job market over the years. The gains were far from earthshaking, but they were a step in the right direction, a step toward achieving equality.

Today, massive layoffs have completely reversed the process. Instead of *preferential hiring,* there is *discriminatory firing* as hundreds of thousands of women and Blacks lose their jobs at a disproportionate rate.

March 1975 statistics from the Department of Labor report that there are 2,760,000 women twenty years old or older who are unemployed. A year ago the figure was 1,586,000. That's a jump of more than one million women out of work, and there are countless others who want and need jobs but have given up looking because they know it is a hopeless search.

The plight of Blacks and other minorities is just as dismal, with an official unemployment rate of 14.2 percent. Among Black teenagers, the unemployment rate is 41.6 percent.

A crucial question facing the labor movement today is how to protect jobs—*particularly the jobs of those bearing the brunt of the layoffs.* A wide debate has erupted around this issue in which the faint-hearted, the fakers, and the fair-weather friends are all showing their true colors.

Conservative labor bureaucrats such as George Meany, head of the AFL-CIO, have made it clear that they couldn't care less about the special plight of women and Black workers. Meany and other top union officials simply hide behind the seniority system.

When asked recently by a reporter if he didn't think some provision should be made for those who were only hired recently, Meany responded, "I stand by the contracts, and I'm sure that's part of our American setup, to stand by your contracts." In other words, to hell with women and Blacks.

The apologists for this racist position complain that any special consideration for Blacks or women is "divisive." But in reality it is Meany's position that plays right into the hands of the bosses, who are using layoffs based on strict seniority to divide the workers. Let's look at what seniority really means.

The seniority system is a limited gain of the union movement, and it has both positive and negative aspects. Fought for and won in the 1930s, seniority prevents the boss—to some degree—from firing whomever he pleases, thus protecting union militants and others the employers consider "troublemakers." Seniority also protects—to some degree—the older workers, whom employers would often like to replace with younger people that they could have work harder and could pay less.

This limited degree of control the unions have won over hiring and firing through the seniority system is valuable and should not be surrendered.

Perpetuates discrimination

But there is another side to seniority. The plain fact is that when women and minorities have been frozen out of jobs and promotions for decades by discrimination, strict seniority can be used to *preserve and perpetuate that discrimination.* It can be used to uphold the relative privileges of white, male workers in opposition to the aspirations of women and Blacks.

That is precisely how the bosses are using the seniority system today.

The labor movement must reject this divisive technique. Labor's answer should be: "We will use the seniority system the way *we* want it used. We are not hypocrites. Unless the gains made by the most oppressed sections of the working class through preferential hiring are now defended, they are meaningless. Unless those advances are protected, Blacks and women will have taken one step forward and two steps backward by the time the bosses are through with them."

Several different proposals have been made for protecting at least some job gains without destroying the positive features of the seniority system. None of them is a substitute for a massive labor offensive against *all* the layoffs. None of them is the answer for every situation or can be applied universally.

But they point in the right direction and are the kinds of answers that should be championed by the union movement.

Preferential seniority

One proposal is that recently hired women and Blacks be given preferential seniority. That is, although only recently hired, they would automatically be given a higher seniority rating as partial compensation for past discrimination and as partial protection against layoffs.

This is only fair. It is hardly the fault of Blacks and women that they are the last hired, so they should not be forced to suffer under the "last hired, first fired" rule.

Special seniority provisions are not new to the union movement. Ever since World War II, for example, some unions have guaranteed men drafted into war their jobs upon return. In addition to their jobs, they were given the seniority they would have earned had they not been drafted.

Another proposal is to insist that layoffs cannot be used to reduce the percentage of women or Blacks in a particular workplace. In other words, this means preserving a minimum quota of jobs for Blacks and women. It is based on the same consideration as preferential seniority: that discrimination in hiring should not be intensified by having women and Blacks be the first fired.

Another valuable demand is for plant-wide seniority rather than seniority by department or job category. This measure can reduce somewhat the vulnerability of women and Blacks to layoffs, since they often have lengthy plant-wide seniority but have only recently moved into better-paying job categories.

By themselves, these steps would be inadequate. They are useful only as a partial solution to discrimination within the broader context of a massive, united labor fight against *all* the layoffs.

The goal of jobs for all can only be won through the organized power of the union movement. The key demands are for an emergency public works program to provide millions of useful jobs at union wages, and for a shorter workweek with no reduction in pay.

The trap, however, lies in counterposing the fight to stop the layoffs with the fight to end discrimination. They are not counterposed, but go hand in hand.

Winning jobs for all is a big task. It will require the united strength of all sections of the working class, and the unions should strive to overcome the divisions that exist. They need to win the support and allegiance of young people, the unemployed, women, and Blacks and other minorities. That can never be done by upholding racist and sexist privileges, but only by being the most stalwart fighters against discrimination.

To say we must demand jobs for all *instead of* defending the gains made by women and Blacks is ducking the issue—at best. Special consideration for women and Blacks, this argument goes, means *accepting* some layoffs. This hypocritical stance ignores one simple fact: so long as the labor movement has not mustered the power to win jobs for all, there *will* be layoffs. Insisting that strict seniority is a sacred principle means accepting some layoffs too—layoffs based on racist and sexist discrimination.

Preferential hiring was and is necessary to begin to compensate for the effects of discrimination and move toward real equality. By the same token, within the overall fight against the layoffs, special steps and special consideration must be given to women and minorities so they are not forced to suffer disproportionately.

Those who were not talking out of both sides of their mouth when supporting preferential hiring will now follow through and demand that the job gains of women and Blacks not be rolled back by discriminatory layoffs.

These questions are now under discussion within the Coalition of Labor Union Women (CLUW). As a union women's organization dedicated to ending the discrimination faced by women in the union, on the job, and in society as a whole, CLUW can play an especially valuable role.

Through panels, seminars, and literature, CLUW can first of all prepare its own members to fight within the union movement for a clear stance against discriminatory layoffs.

Second, it can begin to educate broad sections of the labor movement about the need to defend the hard-won gains of women and minorities.

Third, by setting an example on this issue, CLUW can take another step toward becoming the kind of organization that women, especially Black women, will look to as an unswerving defender of equality.

THE NAACP AND THE STRUGGLE FOR FULL EQUALITY

By Herbert Hill

Herbert Hill is the national labor director of the National Association for the Advancement of Colored People. These are excerpts from his address to a workshop on affirmative action at the July 1975 NAACP convention held in Washington, D.C.

For Black workers, and indeed for the entire Black community, the civil rights issue now is the job issue. What is a recession for whites has become a catastrophic depression for Black workers. As a result of traditional patterns of employment discrimination, Blacks are more vulnerable to long-term economic dislocation than any other group in American society. And many of the gains made during the past twenty years are being rapidly wiped out.

Official government reports on the unemployment crisis tell us that the Black unemployment rate is more than double that of white unemployment. But bad as they are, official unemployment figures are just the tip of the iceberg and the true condition of Black workers is obscured.

• In the major areas of urban Black population concentration the rate of unemployment for Black workers is not merely double but in some instances *four times* greater than the jobless rate among whites.

• Blacks make up 30 percent of those living in officially defined poverty—three times their proportion of the total population.

• In 1970, Black family income for the nation was 61 percent of white family income—the all-time high! In 1971, it dropped to 60 percent, in 1972 to 59 percent, and in 1973 to 58 percent. And every indication is that this downward trend continues.

• At the beginning of 1975 the unemployment rate for white local government workers was 1.7 percent; the unemployment rate for Black local government workers was 11.2 percent—more than *six times* the rate for whites.

• In every industry, in every sector of the economy, Blacks bear the greatest burden of unemployment and endure the heaviest deprivation. Of the greatest significance is the fact that the highest rate of unemployment among all categories is now experienced by Black teen-agers and young workers—in excess of *50 percent*. This obviously means that at least half of the young Black population is in a *permanent* condition of hopelessness and despair and that the social and psychological costs in wasted lives constitutes a major tragedy in contemporary American life.

It is within this context that we must understand the growing nationwide campaign against Black workers and their families. The shrill and paranoid attacks against affirmative-action programs are the cutting edge of the new racism. Given the incontrovertible data on the rapid deterioration of the economic status of Black wage earners; given the fact that Black people suffer the unequal burden of joblessness; given the growing despair and misery in the ghettos of America, the strident shouts of "reverse racism" are based on a totally false assumption. It is another example of the big lie technique; repeat a falsehood long enough and loud enough until so many fools believe it that it becomes an unquestioned "fact."

Gains being erased

The effort to eliminate the present effects of past discrimination, to right the wrongs of many generations, was barely underway when it was aborted. And now, even the very modest gains made by Black men and women through affirmative-action programs are being erased, as powerful institutions turn the clock of history back to the dark and dismal days of "separate but equal."

Judging by the vast outcry, it might be assumed that the use of goals and timetables to eliminate racist job patterns has become as widespread and destructive as discrimination itself. As with the much-distorted subject of busing, the defenders of the racist system have once again succeeded in confusing the remedy with the original evil. The word "quota," like "busing" and "open housing," has become another code word for resistance to demands for the elimination of widespread patterns of discrimination based on race.

The extensive body of case law under Title VII of the Civil Rights Act of 1964 has clearly transformed the negative duty—not to discriminate—into a positive obligation. Under the guise of defending "merit systems" that in reality do not exist, the opponents of affirmative action are, in fact, attempting to maintain the unstated but traditional discriminatory practices that result in the exclusion of Blacks and other minorities from desirable jobs in every sector of the economy. A major factor in the resistance to new legal remedies is that white expectations based on the systematic denial of the rights of minorities has become the norm. Thus any alteration of this norm is considered "reverse discrimination."

It should be evident that what is really involved in the debate over affirmative action is not that Blacks will be given preference over whites but that a substantial body of law now requires that discriminatory systems which operate to favor whites at the expense of Blacks must be eliminated.

This leads us to the burning issue of the moment. That is, the validity of "last hired, first fired" seniority provisions in collective bargaining agreements. In legal terms, the issue may be stated as follows: Is it lawful to invoke seniority as the basis for furlough and dismissal where its application has a disparate impact on Blacks, women, or other minorities. In practical terms, the question is whether those groups that have benefited from Title VII litigation will be forced back into the discriminatory job patterns which existed prior to the enforcement of the Civil Rights Act of 1964. In effect, will the gains of the past decade now be wiped out as a result of traditional seniority procedures codified in union contracts?

There are some who argue that seniority is a vested right. This, of course, is sheer nonsense. The argument that white men have a prior right to a job and that Black people must wait until there is full employment before they too can work is the essence of the racist mentality.

A prime example of resistance to Title VII requirements is to be found in the response of the United Steelworkers of America, a major industrial union. In 1970, after many years of protest by Black steelworkers, a federal court found the steelworkers union and the Bethlehem Steel Corporation in Lackawanna, New York, to be in violation of the law. In *United States* v. *Bethlehem Steel Corp.,* the court stated:

"The pervasiveness and longevity of the overt discriminatory hiring and job assignment practices, admitted by Bethlehem and the union, compel the conclusion that the present seniority and transfer provisions were based on past discriminatory classifications. . . . Job assignment practices were reprehensible. Over 80 percent of black workers were placed in eleven departments which contained the hotter and dirtier jobs in the plant. Blacks were excluded from higher paying and cleaner jobs."

On October 14, 1971, the court issued a decree defining as members of the affected class some 1,600 Black steelworkers who were entitled to receive benefits as a result of the court's decision.

After a decade of litigation under Title VII, it is absolutely clear that seniority provisions in union contracts that perpetuate the present effects of past discrimination are illegal. The Supreme Court in *Griggs* v. *Duke Power* established that intent is irrelevant and that neutral principles which have the effect of continuing discriminatory patterns must be substantially modified or eliminated. It may be anticipated that Black workers, women, and other minorities will make a sustained attack on contractual seniority systems which have a disparate effect and that attempts by employers and organized labor to ward off judicial interference will be futile. In the several decided cases on the "last hired, first fired" issue the law is in conflict. Given the contradictory results in the decided cases and the crucial importance of the issue, this controversy will, of necessity, have to be decided by the Supreme Court. It will have an opportunity to do so in *Franks* v. *Bowman Transportation Co.,* which the court agreed to review on March 24, 1975. This case was initiated by two Black men who had been discharged by the Bowman Transportation Company in Atlanta. Also named as defendant is the collective bargaining agent, the United Steelworkers of America.

Despite the current well-organized political campaign in defense of the "last hired, first fired" principle by corporate enterprise and organized labor, the NAACP will continue the struggle to fully realize the promise of equality contained in the Civil Rights Act of 1964. The association will do this in the courts and outside the courts. And what we are fighting for is grounded on the basic principles of justice.

In the cases in which we are currently involved, Black men and women were systematically denied jobs until major corporations were threatened with lawsuits under Title VII. With the operation of the "last in, first out" principle, the recently employed Black workers are, naturally, the first to be dismissed. Thus, Black workers are doubly penalized. So we are now proposing in the courts that at the very least—as a minimum—that wherever furlough or dismissals occur, the same proportion of nonwhites be retained on the job as existed prior to the layoff.

It is absolutely essential that whatever gains were made, that however modest the toehold, we do not yield. Because it must be understood that those jobs taken from Black men and women today will belong to white men and women tomorrow. And as history teaches us, tomorrow is a very long time.

This struggle involves the fundamental interests of the Black community for many years to come and, therefore, is a crucial issue for the NAACP. And what makes the NAACP unique is that we never subordinate the vital interests of the Black population to other concerns. For us there can be no "other" considerations because for the NAACP there is only one basic responsibility—advancing the interests and welfare of Black Americans. Given the racism which permeates so much of our country we need make no apology for this perception of our role.

We know that if the NAACP does not do it, no one else will. And if we fail, then the future of Black Americans will be nothing more than a dismal repetition of the past. With your help, our just and honest cause will prevail.

THE AFL-CIO AND THE SENIORITY SYSTEM

By Frank Lovell

The AFL-CIO Executive Council issued an official statement in May 1975 on "Seniority and Layoffs." As expected, the statement insists that the seniority system is "a cornerstone of the American labor movement" and rejects out of hand any allowances "to prevent the disproportionate layoff of minority employes."

This stance is a thinly disguised attack on the gains of the civil rights movement and the women's liberation movement in their fight against discriminatory hiring.

Under Title VII of the 1964 Civil Rights Act, employers have in recent years been forced to hire some women and some Blacks and other minority workers for previously all-male or all-white posts. These newly hired workers are now the first fired in the wave of layoffs caused by the worldwide capitalist depression, and they are demanding some protection against being disproportionately victimized.

The basic issue is *defending the equal right to a job for women and minorities.* In the past, preferential hiring, affirmative action, and quotas were the necessary means to begin to compensate for discrimination and move toward equality. In this period of drastic layoffs, it is also a question of affording some special protection so that these workers are not subjected to discriminatory layoffs.

The issue of jobs, seniority, and discrimination is being hotly debated at all levels of the labor and Black movements and in women's organizations. It is of crucial importance for the Coalition of Black Trade Unionists and the Coalition of Labor Union Women, organizations formed for the express purpose of defending the interests of these most oppressed workers. (For story on May 23-26 CBTU convention, see page 13.)

At a recent national conference of the A. Philip Randolph Institute, held in Baltimore, Bayard Rustin, president of the institute, led off a drive to win Black support for the position of the AFL-CIO bureaucracy.

Rustin also traveled to a National Urban League meeting May 23, 1975, in Los Angeles, where he "harshly attacked those civil rights groups which have filed legal actions to protect recently-hired blacks and other minorities and women from being fired because of the current recession," according to a report in the *Los Angeles Times.*

The AFL-CIO tops have decided to promote a witch-hunt against Herbert Hill, the NAACP's labor director, who has been outspoken in criticizing the union bureaucracy's dismal record on job discrimination.

At the Randolph Institute meeting, William Pollard of the AFL-CIO's Civil Rights Department denounced Hill as "irresponsible" and urged union officials to join the NAACP, "get elected to office, go to conventions, and challenge his irresponsibility."

Fact and fancy

The AFL-CIO statement aims to conceal its reactionary apology for discrimination through several debater's tricks. First, it claims that "the seniority system is being blamed for social conditions, particularly discrimination in hiring, that it did not cause."

Who blames the seniority system for discrimination in hiring? This is not specified. Discriminatory hiring is a long-established practice by the employers, going back centuries in fact, and union officials have done little or nothing to correct it.

This false posing of the question dodges the real problem: In those cases where years of discrimination have maintained all-white or all-male departments and job classifications, with a few women and Blacks recently hired, layoffs by strict seniority will serve to *reestablish the discriminatory pattern.*

Seniority does not *cause* discriminatory hiring, but it can *perpetuate its effects.* This obvious fact is resolutely ignored by the AFL-CIO apologists.

"We reject the spurious notion that the seniority system must be destroyed," declares the AFL-CIO top officialdom, "just when it is needed most to protect all workers, without regard to race or sex."

Retention of affirmative-action programs that attack discriminatory hiring and require women and minority workers on all jobs does not destroy the seniority system, and fighters for Black and women's rights have never demanded its destruction.

They *do* call for adjustments so that those who have been hired under these affirmative-action plans (who would never have been hired otherwise) will retain their jobs in direct proportion to the total number of workers employed on any job site.

Contrary to the AFL-CIO portrayal of seniority as a miracle cure for all ills, the seniority system does not and was never intended to "protect all workers." It *sometimes* protects *some* workers, those who have been longest on the job. Even this is by no means strictly enforced. The employers have always devised ways of circumventing the seniority system, creating exceptions, when it served their purposes to do so—usually with the approval and collaboration of union officials.

In cases where "strict seniority" is applied, the "last hired is first fired." As a general rule this applies to women, Blacks, and others who were discriminated against in the hiring process. So most of these workers have *no* protection under the seniority system.

There are hardly any instances where Blacks or women have top seniority. In some work departments that hire only women or Blacks (the dirtiest, lowest-paying, and most menial), seniority provides no more protection against layoffs than anywhere else. Often whole departments are closed, and those workers with high seniority cannot carry their seniority to other departments of the plant unless they are protected by an affirmative-action program that requires the employer to transfer them out of their previous segregated positions.

Far from protecting "all workers," the seniority system as it has operated in the past is a way of determining *preferential treatment.* This is defended by Meany and his cohorts in the AFL-CIO statement. "The American workers," it says, "regardless of race, do not think it inequitable that the more senior workers are protected in times of layoff, nor would they think it equitable that those workers be forced to surrender a portion of work to junior employes whose needs may be less, whose opportunities for securing other employment are greater, and whose investment of labor in the enterprise has been shorter."

There is nothing "equitable" about mass layoffs, and the AFL-CIO hierarchy will never convince the American workers that there is. Workers who are laid off—young and old alike—find nothing "fair" about it.

Nor is it possible to convince Blacks and women that they are suddenly, in the economic crisis, receiving "equal treatment" because, as the labor skates assert, "according to Commissioner of Labor Statistics Julius Shiskin, the best evidence available is that white male workers and black male workers have been hit by layoffs about the same in the current recession, and that men have been hit harder by layoffs than women."

That is certainly no consolation to laid-off white workers. And try telling it to those women and Blacks who have lost their jobs and have no prospect of finding any!

"We repeat," concludes the AFL-CIO argument for seniority, "what we have often said: Full employment is the only solution to unemployment and to discrimination. And we will not stand idly by while a few would pit worker against worker for the right to be employed."

The right to be employed! This right to employment is what is under attack, not the seniority system. Every worker has the right to a job, but the fact is that more than 11 million are deprived of that right today by the capitalist system.

This right should be championed by the union movement, not in pious truisms like "full employment is the only solution to unemployment" (anybody knows that), but in organized struggle against the employers and their hired politicians, who are handing out the dismissal slips.

In the absence of such a fight, all talk about full employment being the answer to discrimination is a shabby cover-up for *acceptance of the racism and sexism of discriminatory firing.*

A massive federal public works program is surely necessary to "put America back to work." There is no lack of work to be done to build mass-transit systems, low-cost public housing, hospitals, schools, and libraries. Huge projects ought to be undertaken to clean up the polluted streams and lakes, reclaim vast reaches of destroyed land, and reforest barren hillsides.

All this is a far cry from the piddling one million "make work" public service jobs the AFL-CIO lobbyists are asking Congress to provide with a $10 billion appropriation.

What about the other 10 million unemployed workers? Don't they have enough seniority to qualify for jobs? What hiring system will determine who deserves the one million public service jobs, if and when Congress appropriates the money for them? Will not this "pit worker against worker for the right to be employed"?

There is an additional way the AFL-CIO could create jobs for millions now out of work if it were serious about the fight. In 1932 a bill was introduced in Congress by Senator Hugo Black for a thirty-hour workweek. It was passed by the U.S. Senate.

Technological advances and greatly increased labor productivity during the intervening forty-three years make the thirty-hour workweek with no reduction in pay a social and economic necessity today. Why is it that not one of the many "friends of labor," elected with union money, has yet thought to introduce legislation in the present Congress for a thirty-hour workweek?

The hours of work can be shortened with no reduction in pay.

A massive public works program can be started.

The union movement ought to champion these demands and mobilize the working class—the unorganized, the unemployed, the youth, all the poor—to win them.

This would require a serious effort and *demonstrated good intentions* to unite all workers behind these demands. Right now it is the reactionary position of the AFL-CIO bureaucracy in defending the status quo of discrimination that pits worker against worker and cripples the fight for jobs, not the just demands of the oppressed for equality.

The union movement badly needs to show that it is able and willing to defend the rights—especially the "right to be employed"—of those most cruelly discriminated against and most vulnerable to victimization and exploitation by unscrupulous employers.

There is no better time and no better place to start than now in support of the affirmative-action programs that have been won. These affirmative-action programs, which make room in the work force for women, Blacks, and others previously excluded from many jobs, are big gains for the union movement and should be defended and extended.

There are several instances where these gains are challenged and are in danger of being wiped out. A few examples will suffice:

• **AT&T:** The Bell System telephone companies failed to comply with the agreement they signed in 1973 to end their employment discrimination. The government has now brought action against these companies and the parent American Telephone and Telegraph Company to force them to compensate victimized workers to the tune of around $2.5 million.

They were discovered to have given 10,000 fewer new jobs and promotions to previously discriminated-against groups than they should have if they had lived up to their 1973 affirmative-action agreement.

The discovery of AT&T's discriminatory practices was made by government agencies, not the Communication Workers of

America, which is the union involved and is partly responsible for the discrimination.

The corporation has agreed to new antidiscrimination standards and procedures, signed by the Equal Employment Opportunity Commission, the Department of Labor, the Justice Department, and the General Services Administration.

The court order putting the new standards into effect was held up by a challenge by the CWA, which claims its contracts are being violated. These contracts were written in compliance with company discrimination, and in this case the union is simply fronting for the company to maintain the discriminatory practices. This is a repeat of the disgraceful CWA challenge to the 1973 affirmative-action agreement, which it lost, although AT&T continued to violate the agreement anyway.

• **The Steel trust:** Another highly publicized case is in the steel industry, which discriminated against Blacks by assigning them to the dirtiest, most hazardous jobs, and kept them in those positions through a system of departmental seniority. The result was all-Black and all-white units, and no crossing of departmental lines. This "seniority system" was written into the union contract.

Nearly all jobs in the mills were closed to women workers until Blacks and women forced the Justice Department to bring legal action. The Steelworkers union did not support these actions, but last year after the case was won, Steelworkers President I.W. Abel and the nine major steel companies signed a consent decree allowing "plantwide seniority."

This permits many Black workers to move up into classifications that were previously closed to them. The decree also protects the steel companies by limiting back pay for the years of discrimination. Here, again, the union served the needs of the employers and did nothing either to protect or unite the workers on this issue.

• **Jersey Central Power and Light Co.:** The recent case of the Jersey Central Power and Light Company is a clear example of how discrimination is used to divide the workers and weaken the union. This company was found guilty of discriminatory hiring and was forced to comply with an affirmative-action program, which resulted in the placement of women and some minorities.

When the company decided to lay off about 10 percent of its total 3,850-member work force, it went to the courts for guidance. A federal judge ordered a reduction of the work force in a way that would not disproportionately victimize the newly hired minorities.

In other words, two categories of workers would be recognized: those hired as a result of the court-ordered affirmative actions, and those previously hired under *discriminatory* company practices.

If the total work force were to be reduced by one-tenth, then one of every ten workers in each group would be laid off in line of group seniority. A formula like this does not stop the layoffs. But it does guarantee equal treatment to victims of previous discrimination.

This ruling was overturned last January by an appeals court in Philadelphia, which ruled that "the provisions of the collective bargaining agreement must govern."

The appeal was brought by bureaucrats of the International Brotherhood of Electrical Workers, AFL-CIO, which had not done much to halt the layoffs but was quick to enter the case in order to scuttle the gains against discrimination.

In handing down its decision, the appeals court put the onus of discrimination on the union, not the company, where it properly belongs.

Working-class unity

The long-term effects of intervention by unions like those cited will deepen the existing divisions within the working class and render these unions powerless to protect the privileges of their remaining members, much less wage the more difficult fight for full employment.

The real meaning of the statement of the AFL-CIO Executive Council on seniority is clearly a declaration in support of discrimination against women and Black workers as practiced by most corporations, having nothing to do with protection of jobs or working-class solidarity.

The statement can have no other purpose, in view of the council's record against affirmative-action programs and the failure of the union movement to organize and educate against discrimination in employment.

At the previously mentioned conference of the A. Philip Randolph Institute in Baltimore, May 17-19, Bayard Rustin said that he was opposed to "gimmicks" in attempting to deal with "real economic questions affecting the majority of Blacks." He added that "this effort to tamper with our seniority system is also a gimmick."

This conference was one of seven similar meetings that have been held recently under the auspices of the AFL-CIO-subsidized Randolph Institute. The announced purposes of these conferences are to train Blacks in voter registration and to recruit Blacks for government-financed apprenticeship programs. The problems they encounter are: no suitable candidates for Blacks to vote for, no jobs for Black apprentices in the skilled trades, and discrimination against Blacks in jobs and training wherever they turn.

In the face of these facts, Rustin's defense of "seniority" in relation to the "real economic questions" has all the earmarks of gimmickry—in addition to the more sinister intent behind it.

The gains for the AFL-CIO position against the fight to eliminate discrimination in employment are that these conferences always turn up a few Blacks who are willing to put themselves on record for "seniority" without realizing that this issue is being used to scuttle affirmative-action programs. Rustin and others like him then report this as the representative opinion of "Black workers"—all of them solidly in support of "strict seniority."

Of course, there are always some dissenters, even at the carefully organized conferences of the A. Philip Randolph Institute. A twenty-four-year-old Baltimore carpenter, George Jones, who must have been invited by accident, said at the local conference there that he is "a militant getting more militant as things get worse."

Rustin's response to this was to say that such feelings will abate as the economy improves.

There are a few million young Black workers like George Jones who see no sign of improvement, not for them anyway. Those without jobs or just hired because of the Civil Rights Act see no advantage in "seniority." They need jobs now, and seniority does not create jobs.

Meanwhile, the AFL-CIO bureaucracy is maneuvering to impose its narrow-minded and reactionary position on the Coalition of Black Trade Unionists, the Coalition of Labor Union Women, and other Black and union organizations. An endorsement of the AFL-CIO statement on the false issue of "strict seniority"—"in principle," of course—by these organizations would have some short-range propaganda value for the bureaucracy in its present attack on affirmative-action programs.

But that would be a blow to the interests of the union movement and of all workers. The unions will never succeed in organizing the unorganized, or in leading a powerful movement against unemployment, inflation, and the other evils of this system, so long as their leaders allow themselves to be used to keep women and minorities down.

WHERE SOCIALIST CANDIDATES STAND ON DISCRIMINATORY LAYOFFS

A Discussion with Willie Mae Reid

The following exchange is based on the discussion period at a campaign rally held in June 1975 by Willie Mae Reid, Socialist Workers party candidate for vice-president of the United States.

Question: Many Blacks and women have been hired, or moved into higher-paying jobs, in the last few years through affirmative-action plans that they fought for. Now, through the "last hired, first fired" practice, they are being fired first in the layoffs. Some of them say that they think this is unfair and say they should not be the first fired. Do you think they are right?

Reid: Absolutely right. If the affirmative-action gains can just be wiped out under the seniority system when times get tough, then they didn't mean much, did they?

Look at what this means. When women and Blacks forced the bosses to hire and upgrade them, it was a victory over racism and discrimination against women. It was also a step forward for the whole labor movement. Why? Because it weakened one of the bosses' weapons—dividing the working class and pitting Black against white and male against female. It cut across the notion that Blacks and women don't deserve jobs, that we are expendable.

Now, the bosses are taking advantage of the layoffs to *further divide* working people, by firing Blacks and women first and taking back what we have won. The bosses gain by this, not the workers.

Question: So you think they should fire the white male workers first?

Reid: No. What I'm saying is that the bosses shouldn't be allowed to use the layoffs to reduce the percentage of women and Blacks. That's all. The *percentage* of women and Blacks in the work force—won through struggle—should be maintained.

Look. If a factory was 90 percent white and 10 percent Black before layoffs, and is still those same percentages after the layoffs, then Blacks have not been disproportionately affected. Right?

But that's not what's happening. In many places the percentage of Blacks and women is being *reduced.* Blacks and women are being disproportionately laid off. That's discrimination and that's what I'm against.

Take the example of Continental Can Company in Harvey, Louisiana. They laid off 200 workers, including 48 of the 50 Black workers at the plant. All but two of the Black workers had been hired since 1965. Now, some of the Black workers there went to court and said that the fact that they didn't have as much seniority as the whites was because of the boss's racist hiring policy. They said they shouldn't have to continue to pay the price of discrimination.

The judge ruled that some of the Black workers had to be rehired—enough so that the percentage of Blacks in the factory was the same after the layoffs as before. I think the judge was right, don't you?

Question: Yes, I do. It's true that your proposal would knock out the discriminatory aspect of the layoffs. But there's still a problem. People are still being laid off.

Reid: Absolutely true. There's still an enormous problem. It's a different problem: how to stop the layoffs and provide everyone with a job.

I have a proposal for that, too. To stop the layoffs and provide jobs for all we need to shorten the workweek with no reduction in pay. We also need a government-funded massive public works program to provide useful jobs.

That's what I propose. But, unfortunately, what I propose isn't being implemented yet. And we have to deal with the fact that there *are* massive layoffs taking place, and the layoffs *are* hitting Blacks and women first and hitting us hardest. Now, I'm against the discriminatory aspect of the layoffs that are taking place—and that's what this whole fight by women and Blacks to protect their gains is all about. It's about fighting discrimination.

The union movement has to carry out a fight on both fronts. It has to fight against the discriminatory aspects of the current layoffs and it has to fight for jobs for all.

Remember, for many, many years Blacks and women have been locked out of many jobs, of the best jobs.

Companies refused to hire us. And, with all too few exceptions, the unions have gone along with this. Some unions became the enforcers of this discrimination policy. The bosses used reactionary prejudices of many workers to keep the working class divided.

We had to fight the companies and the union bureaucrats to win affirmative-action plans. Now, it seems obvious to me, those gains must be *defended.*

Question: O.K. But won't the white workers who get laid off be resentful?

Reid: Anybody that gets laid off is going to be resentful! Period. And no one is more resentful than women and Blacks. We have been resentful for a long time about being laid off first. If resentment could guarantee a job, we'd all be working.

The issue is this: how can we deal with the bosses to make the attacks they are now carrying out against the working masses as a whole as ineffective as possible? And that means uniting the working class. That can not be done by surrendering to the backwardness of white workers at the expense of Blacks and women.

And I'll tell you something else. If the union movement would unite in defense of the gains of Blacks and women, it would strengthen the unions for other fights—such as the fight for a shorter workweek. It would make it possible for the unions to take on other fights *united.*

EXPERIENCES OF A WOMAN STEELWORKER

By Sue Em Davenport

In August 1975, I and three other unemployed women steelworkers from the Homestead mill in Pittsburgh met with local officials of the United Steelworkers union to enlist their help in getting our jobs back. It was an instructive experience.

We realized that as part of the "last hired, first fired" category of American workers, we were going to have an uphill battle with U.S. Steel. But we came away from the meeting with a flavor for what we're up against in our own union as well.

Production at the Homestead mill has been cut back nearly 17 percent, but almost 95 percent of the women who were employed in traditionally nonfemale jobs have been laid off.

The four of us who attended this meeting, plus several others who were unable to come, feel that these layoffs are discriminatory to women. The steel industry has been one of the most reluctant to open its doors to women, and most of the women at Homestead were hired only after the so-called consent decree went into effect in April 1974. Some of the women had persistently applied at area steel mills for up to seven years before then.

The first step toward retrieving our jobs was to file a grievance with the union, but it was refused. Under the contract and the consent decree, they said, we had no legitimate grievance.

So we moved on to file a complaint with the union's Civil Rights Committee. We set up a meeting with the head of that committee, and he in turn invited the entire committee, the local president, and our staff representative. Everyone chose to attend except the staff representative.

We hoped that the meeting would produce a commitment from the local to back us up in our fight to regain our jobs.

We explained how gains that women had made through affirmative-action programs were now being wiped out. Our position, we said, is that under no circumstances should the percentage of women at the mill be reduced during layoffs. We didn't insist on exactly how that demand should be implemented. But we did offer some alternatives that are being considered elsewhere, such as dual seniority.

Dual seniority provides for two seniority lists: one for workers hired under affirmative-action programs and one list for other workers. During a cutback, layoffs would be made in equal percentages from both lists.

Our discussion with the union officials revolved around the question of seniority. They maintained that seniority is not only a principle of trade unionism, but a sacred institution. Without seniority, they said, the bosses could "cherry pick" to their hearts' content, and no one would have any protection against the whims of the employer.

While we agreed that seniority does protect some workers, it wasn't protecting us. In fact, it was maintaining past discrimination.

They said layoffs were the company's prerogative under the Basic Steel Contract, and that the union has no power to fight the layoffs unless they violate plant-wide seniority.

How did we think male steelworkers who had also been laid off would feel, they asked us, if the union helped us get our jobs back while they were still on the streets? We answered that the men would expect the union to get their jobs back too. Wasn't that a reasonable thing for them to expect? They appeared uneasy about that response.

They just couldn't help, they told us, but maybe we could set up a meeting with a representative from the union's international office. After all, they argued, it is the international that makes all the decisions, not the locals.

Throughout the meeting they indicated that they did not consider women to be a minority with special problems within the union. This was particularly apparent when we raised our desire to become more active in the local.

Could we have a woman representative on the Civil Rights Committee or elsewhere? No, committee appointments were made on the basis of support for the "right" people during the last local election. And there were no vacancies on any committees. Besides, there are 5,000 men in the local who would like to be on committees; why should they appoint a woman?

The next local elections will be in April 1976. There will be no woman in the entire local eligible to run under the present requirements that candidates have two years' service plus a record of attendance at two-thirds of the local meetings.

We have filed complaints with both the Equal Employment Opportunity Commission and the Pennsylvania Human Relations Committee. We have asked our union to join us as a party to the suit. With or without them, we're going to fight.

TWO TESTS FOR THE SENIORITY SYSTEM: THE MACHINISTS OF NASHVILLE AND THE UAW'S 'BACK PAY-FRONT PAY' SCHEME

By Linda Jenness

The issue of protecting the affirmative-action gains of women and Blacks in the face of massive layoffs may sometimes appear abstract. But the stark conflict between entrenched white privilege and Black demands for equality is shown in real-life terms in two Nashville, Tennessee, plants.

The issues are clear and the lines are sharply drawn at Ford Motor Company's glass plant and at AVCO Corporation, an aerospace subcontractor. Large layoffs have hit both plants.

Ford Glass was almost lily-white before 1964. So was United Auto Workers Local 737, the union there. But in 1964 Congress passed the Civil Rights Act, which outlawed job discrimination on the basis of race and sex. And in the years following, Black workers fought to break down the color line.

By the end of 1970, Black workers had gotten about 15 percent of the jobs at Ford Glass—about the same proportion as in the overall Nashville work force.

Then came the layoffs. Laying off on a strict seniority basis—last in, first out—Ford Glass cut its work force by 25 percent. That included, however, *60 percent* of the Black workers—200 out of the 350 Blacks. Another round of layoffs, expected by almost everyone at the plant, would eliminate most of the remaining Black workers.

An article in the August 3, 1975, *Washington Post* by John Egerton, entitled "Black vs. White on Who Gets Ax," tells of the differing views about what should be done.

"I hope the Blacks don't get a wild hair and try this 'instant seniority' stuff," said one white worker with twenty years' seniority at the Ford plant. "If they do, all hell's gonna break loose."

A Black worker with nine years' seniority who has been laid off since January sees things a little differently. "If things don't get better, I see a disaster for Black people, for America," he said. "Something's gonna have to be done, or there'll be hell to pay."

Most of the white workers at Ford Glass view any move to alter the seniority provisions with open hostility. Some of the Black workers, on the other hand, think alterations have to be made. "Seniority is okay," said one, "but still it's wrong to turn every Black man out in the street."

The clash is even more sharply expressed at the AVCO Corporation plant in Nashville.

One of the first racial discrimination suits filed after passage of the 1964 Civil Rights Act was brought against AVCO by a Black worker. And Blacks have had to continually fight both the company and the union to be hired and upgraded since then. Workers at AVCO are organized by Local 735 of the International Association of Machinists.

A few historical facts about the International Association of Machinists help put the conflict in perspective. For sixty of its eighty-plus years of existence, IAM barred "non-Caucasians" from membership.

During World War II the Machinists locals, along with the International Brotherhood of Boilermakers, were particularly notorious for their racist practices. They actively opposed the employment and upgrading of Blacks whenever and however possible.

When forced to admit Blacks, they relegated them to second-class status. In some cases Blacks were issued only thirty-day work permits by the union, were charged higher initiation fees and dues, and then received no membership rights in return.

When Black workers at AVCO, as late as the summer of 1975, won a discrimination suit against both the company and Local 735, and the company was forced to hire more Blacks, 500 white workers staged a brief walkout.

"That ruling tore our seniority system all to pieces," claimed the union president. But "seniority" wasn't the issue. Racism was.

Five years ago AVCO employed 4,000 production workers, including more than 500 Blacks, about 13 percent. Today, only 1,700 workers are on the job, less than 9 percent of them Black.

Most white workers at AVCO have been opposed to hiring Blacks all along, so the idea of defending Black gains in the face of layoffs is the furthest thing from their minds.

The president of Local 735 is Jack Bonner. Bonner reflects the views of many of the white members of his local. He believes that the affirmative-action plans were "prejudiced against whites" to begin with.

"Now," says Bonner, "we've got a lot of laid-off people out there trying to survive, and they're getting tired of this equal employment opportunity crap. . . . We've got a lot of turmoil in this country. All you hear is Black power, women's rights, welfare, big profits for the corporations. . . ."

Leon McClain, a Black worker at AVCO with ten years' seniority, puts the blame elsewhere. "I'm a strong believer in unions," says McClain. "But our local is not really for the workers, Black or white."

The union leaders, he charges, "are bleeding the workers—not just Blacks and women but white men, too. Our pay scale is lower than the scale of the big contractors we're doing work for, like Lockheed. We don't have any sick leave benefits. We don't have a supplementary unemployment benefit fund, like they have at Ford Glass. And on top of all that, there's the racial thing."

Protecting 'white rights'

Union President Bonner, however, is convinced that the "equal opportunity crap" is to blame.

Bonner makes no fine distinctions between "equal opportunity crap" in the area of employment and in other areas, such as housing and school desegregation.

In fact, Bonner is organizing a local chapter of ROAR (Restore Our Alienated Rights), the racist outfit that began in Boston around the busing issue and has since spread to other cities and other issues.

ROAR has broken up women's rights actions in Boston. In

Queens, New York, it has organized to force a Black family to move out of a predominantly white neighborhood.

ROAR stands opposed to everything the union movement ought to be fighting for. The unions should fight to protect the most oppressed layers of the working class and pave the way for united working-class action against the bosses.

Bonner's support for ROAR exposes what his defense of the "seniority principle" is all about: pure, unadulterated racism.

These views were summed up in a recent ROAR advertisement in the New York *Daily News,* which read, in part:

"We are tired of watching our mothers and fathers, after long years of seniority, lose their jobs in order to protect those newly-hired 'minorities.' *We are tired* of standing idly by while our brothers and sisters are denied entrance to law and medical schools, in favor of less qualified 'minorities,' and most of all . . . *We are tired* of having our children bussed [sic] out so that 'minority' children may be bussed into our schools."

It's little wonder, then, that the Black workers at the AVCO plant in Nashville charge the union with collaborating with the company to discriminate against them, and turn to the courts for protection.

Leon McClain says, "If the company had been hiring and promoting Blacks fairly since the 1964 law was passed, there wouldn't be any need for lawsuits. But they haven't done that, and they still aren't doing it.

"As far as layoffs are concerned, they've had seniority within each department instead of plant-wide, and when they have to cut back, they hit the departments where the most Blacks are.

"The court says they have to use plant-wide seniority now, but even that still hits Black workers the hardest, because almost all of us were hired after the 1964 law."

The white workers, in their majority, including union President Bonner, say that strict seniority must prevail in the layoffs.

McClain says, "Plant-wide seniority is a fair system if it's done right, but before they let all the Black workers go, I think some consideration ought to be given to the fact that before 1964, Blacks had no rights at all. I don't think it would be right for this plant to go back to an all-white work force."

The two Nashville plants are just examples of a nationwide pattern, and the conflict between strict seniority and affirmative-action gains is the subject of a hot and heavy debate within the union movement.

Do the union leaders agree with Leon McClain that it just wouldn't be right to go back to an all-white work force? Or do they agree with Jack Bonner that it's time to put an end to "equal opportunity crap"? Let's look at some recent stands on this question adopted by the union officialdom.

The outcry by women and Black workers for an end to discriminatory layoffs is making a significant impact in the labor movement. Even the top echelons of the union officialdom have been forced to take notice that wholesale layoffs on a "last hired, first fired" basis are wiping out the equal-employment gains won in the 1960s.

And some officials, under pressure from Blacks and women in their own union ranks—and from court actions by the NAACP—have started to come up with their own "answers" to the problem.

Upon closer examination, however, most of their supposed solutions turn out just to be gimmicks to give the appearance of equal treatment while accepting the status quo of discrimination.

One of the slicker schemes is the "back pay-front pay" plan proposed by officials of the United Auto Workers. "Back pay-front pay" was explained by William Oliver, director of the UAW's Fair Practices Department, to a recent UAW women's conference. It is supposed to be the UAW's alternative to making any changes in the seniority system. Here's how it works—and watch closely, it's tricky.

'Back pay-front pay'

Suppose you are a woman or a Black, and you applied for a particular job in 1965 but you weren't hired. But let's say you applied again for the same job in 1969 and this time you got it. If you can prove that the reason you weren't hired four years earlier was discrimination, the UAW says the company should be forced to pay you for the four years. That's the "back pay" part.

Suppose further that you got laid off in 1973. That, of course, is sooner than you would have been laid off if your seniority was counted from 1965 instead of 1969. So, the UAW officials say, the company should also give you "front pay" from 1973 until the date you would have been laid off if you had seniority from 1965. Is that clear?

In the first place, "back pay-front pay" is currently only an idea in the heads of the UAW officials. It is not clear whether they have even raised it as a demand on the auto companies—much less organized for a fight to win it.

And "back pay-front pay" would be fine for those who could get it—there must be all of half a dozen people in the UAW who would qualify. But what about Blacks and women who can't prove that they applied at a certain time and were discriminated against? After all, how many people keep detailed records of all the places they have ever tried to get work?

What about those who didn't even apply at a particular plant because everybody knew the place didn't hire Blacks? Before the civil rights laws were passed, it could have been not only futile but dangerous to go after a "white man's job."

What about all those women and Blacks who are being laid off by a different company from the one that didn't hire them before?

This whole scheme evades the real issue of discriminatory layoffs. It pretends discrimination is just an *individual* problem that can be solved on an individual basis, rather than a matter of entrenched patterns of racist and sexist discrimination, built up over the years, that affect *all* Blacks and *all* women.

How would the UAW apply "back pay-front pay" to the crisis facing its local at Ford Glass Company in Nashville, which I described earlier?

The problem at UAW Local 737 is not one where a few individuals can "prove" that they applied for their jobs a few years earlier and were turned away. The cold, hard fact is that *60 percent of the Black workers at Ford Glass have been laid off*—far out of proportion to the layoffs suffered by whites. Ford Glass may soon return to being a lily-white plant and Local 737 a lily-white local. What does the UAW officialdom propose to do about that?

The answer is: nothing. The answer is that they couldn't care less. If they did, they would tell Local 737 to get busy and defend its Black members.

They could, for example, draw up two seniority lists—one for the Black workers hired after 1964 (the year Congress outlawed discriminatory hiring) and one for the workers hired previously—and see to it the layoffs are not used to racially discriminate against Blacks by axing them in disproportionate numbers.

Gimmicks such as "back pay-front pay" won't do a thing to protect the UAW's Black and women members—*and the UAW officials know it.* UAW President Leonard Woodcock also addressed the women's conference mentioned above. Equal employment opportunity, he bluntly told the women, "will not be possible without an economy of full employment." In other words, *only after everybody else has a job* can women and Blacks expect equal treatment.

Women and Black workers are all for full employment. But pie-in-the-sky promises are no substitute for *equal treatment now*—especially when the promises come from union bureaucrats who are doing exactly nothing to fight for jobs for all.

Where Meany stands

The same sort of tokenism is endorsed by George Meany and the AFL-CIO Executive Council, the most ardent defenders of strict seniority in layoffs. They have now announced support for a suit by a group of Black workers demanding seniority dating back to their initial job applications with the company where they work.

Meany will support them because they can prove they personally were discriminated against by one particular company. This is supposed to show that Meany is against discrimination.

The AFL-CIO's court brief emphasizes that this case is entirely different from saying that minority or women workers "should be afforded special seniority protections against layoff, not because they themselves have been discriminated against, but because discrimination against others has produced a situation in which preferential protection against layoff is the only way to preserve racial or sexual balance in the workforce."

At its summer session, the AFL-CIO Executive Council passed a resolution warning that "the natural alliance between the labor movement and the civil rights movement" is threatened by "demagogic attacks on the seniority system."

Elsewhere in the union movement there are some signs of more meaningful attention to the problem of discriminatory layoffs. The July convention of the Newspaper Guild voted to explore ways of dealing with layoffs "in a fair and equitable manner that would avoid deterioration of gains that have been achieved for women and minorities."

The International Executive Board of the American Federation of State, County and Municipal Employees, meeting June 30, 1975, adopted a resolution on affirmative action that at least heads in the right direction.

Referring to the destructive results of the layoffs, AFSCME states that "a less visible, but no less unfortunate consequence of public employee layoffs is the erosion of gains which have been made to correct decades of discrimination against women and minorities. . . .

"Senseless layoffs of needed public employees can only lead to a return of the discriminatory abuses of the past."

It continues: "AFSCME, with other unions, is now faced with the imminent possibility that two hard-won principles, seniority and affirmative action, will be eroded as governmental employers follow a disastrous course of decreasing public service in this period of increased public need."

For this reason it is resolved: "That AFSCME will urge its local affiliates to protect against management eroding either the hard-won principle of seniority or the equally hard-won principle of affirmative action through layoffs that are politically motivated, unjustified, or an attempt to return to the discriminatory abuses of the past."

It is unquestionably a step forward to recognize that affirmative action is a principle equal in importance with seniority, and that the layoffs "can only lead to a return of the discriminatory abuses of the past."

The weakness of the resolution lies in its failure to take a firm position against any percentage decrease of women or Blacks in the work force. Instead, the resolution merely calls on AFSCME locals "to review layoffs on a case-by-case basis to insure that layoff procedures are not used as a guise to permit roll-backs of recently initiated affirmative action gains. . . ."

What should be done

The union officials up and down the line profess to be very concerned that the burden of correcting past discrimination not fall on the white, male workers now holding jobs. It should fall on the companies instead, they say. That's a laudable sentiment, shared by most Blacks and women, who are not out to take jobs away from anybody else.

All workers affected by unemployment would rally behind a serious fight launched by the unions to provide jobs for all through a massive public works program and a shorter workweek with no reduction in pay. United labor action to win these demands would be a lot more convincing than all the pious declarations now coming from Meany, Woodcock, and the rest.

Right now the reality is that the *victims* of past discrimination in hiring are the ones being made to suffer, through disproportionate layoffs based on strict seniority.

The unions have an obligation to stand up against these discriminatory layoffs and fight against any percentage decrease of women or Blacks on the job. Where the seniority system comes into conflict with affirmative-action gains, seniority should be modified to protect those gains.

To do so is not only a moral obligation; it is the only way to forge the labor unity necessary to win jobs for all.